Discover True Love
by
Arthur S. Meintjes

All scripture references in King James Version unless otherwise specified.

No part of this publication may be reproduced in any form without the permission of the publisher

A KINGDOM LIFE MINISTRIES PUBLICATION
1777 GORE CREEK CT
WINDSOR CO 80550
Tel: 970 541-0838
www.arthurmeintjes.com
info@arthurmeintjes.com

Published: 2012

About the Author

Arthur is a Bible teacher and conference speaker and has traveled the world teaching the GOOD NEWS (Gospel of Peace) and FAITH-RIGHTEOUSNESS, the message of God's unconditional love, goodness and mercy to restore mankind.

He is also an adjunct lecturer at Charis Bible College in Colorado Springs, Colorado where he teaches first and second year classes for both the day and night school. He teaches third year classes on invitation.

He is a frequent guest speaker at several other CBC campuses in the USA and the United Kingdom.

Arthur has also written a book titled Knowing and Experiencing God and co-authored a book with his wife Cathy titled Grace and Faith Thoughts. He has a lively, passionate and heartfelt teaching style that has touched many hearts and He finds tremendous fulfillment in seeing lives changed and future leaders encouraged to share the gospel of grace and peace in their world. He and Cathy have three children and currently reside in Colorado, USA iv

Discover True Love

Table of Contents

Introduction   vii

1 – Do You Love Me?   1

2 – Love is Of God   23

3 – A Biblical Definition of God's Love 55

4 – God Speaks a Language of Love   83

5 – What is This Language of Love?   101

6 – Learning the Language of Love   113

7 – That we Might Have Life   123

Discover True Love
INTRODUCTION

PURSUE THIS GREAT LOVE!

I Corinthians 13:13: *And so faith, hope, love abide; these three; but the greatest of these is love.*

I Corinthians 14:1: *Eagerly pursue and seek to acquire (this) love (make it your aim, your great quest).*

The Message Bible: Go after a life of love as if your life depended on it – because it does!

The fact that you are alive is a sign that God cares! Your very breath depends on God's love. Everything you need for life and godliness has been given to you by the work of Christ on the cross.

My favorite definition of agape (unconditional) love is that in my weakest, worst moment (and we all know our moments), God sees me as valuable, precious and something to be held in high regard or esteem. That can feel like a tall order to believe! I know what I am like at times. I know what I do, what I believe, what I say that makes me a miserable and sometimes horrible person. Yet agape love doesn't look at that at all. It makes no difference to agape love (God's love). He has placed all His love and acceptance on you through the finished work of the cross.

Don't pursue vain and unimportant things to try and find life. The people around you and the things that we "think" we need for life in this world cannot give us true life. Only the awesome, perfect love of God can give life. Pursue (go after understanding this love) or becoming persuaded of its perfection and you will be a whole person. It's when you find out that someone (God) believes in you that you realize your potential and value. And my friend, God believes in you with all of His heart. In I Corinthians 13:7 we read that love (God is love) is ever ready to believe the best of every person.

In a conference that we held in South Africa several years ago, we had a man and his wife come for prayer saying: "We accepted the truth about the Lord many years ago, but we realize now that the God we accepted is not the one you have been sharing with us. We want to accept the gift of love and acceptance that the gospel of peace offers." This was truly a life-changing time for this couple. We are so privileged to see change in lives everywhere we minister the true, unconditional acceptance of God.

You can experience this change too if you will just let go of your own efforts and accept the already completed gift that God is offering you today. You will not be disappointed!

Discover True Love

Chapter One

Do You Love Me?
(The touching story of Peter and Jesus)

I was on the airplane reading my bible, just relaxing after a successful ministry trip in the USA, reading from the John 21 verse 15 – 17, when the Holy Spirit spoke to me as clearly as I've ever heard Him. He said: "Arthur, do you notice this question that Jesus asked Peter? I said, "Yes Lord". He said, "Most Christians today fear that they might ever be asked this same question.

At first I did not realize what the Lord was trying to communicate to me. But as I started to study this passage of scripture a little closer it hit me like a four-pound hammer against the head.

John 21:15-17 - *So when they had dined, Jesus saith to Simon Peter, Simon, son of Jonas, lovest thou me more than these? He saith unto him, Yea, Lord; thou knowest that I love thee. He saith unto him, Feed my lambs. He saith to him again the second time, Simon, son of Jonas, lovest thou me? He saith unto him, Yea, Lord; thou knowest that I love thee. He saith unto him, Feed my sheep. He saith unto him the third time, Simon, son of Jonas, lovest thou me? Peter was grieved because he said unto him the third time, Lovest thou me? And he said unto him, Lord, thou knowest all things; thou knowest that I love thee. Jesus saith unto him, Feed my sheep.* (KJV)

In order to get a good understanding of what this conversation between Jesus and Peter was all about, we need to backtrack a little. Remember that not long before this incident at the Passover meal Peter was the one who boldly said, "Jesus although all shall be offended, yet will not I," [Mark 14: 29]. You see Peter was just like so many of us today, Peter thought that all it took to follow Jesus and to be a man of God is commitment, discipline and follow-through. So that was exactly what he did, he fervently committed himself and boldly and verbally proclaimed his disciplined commitment.

Simon Peter said to Him, Lord, where are you going? Jesus answered, You are not able to follow Me now where I am going, but you shall follow me afterwards. Peter said to Him, Lord, why cannot I follow you now? I will lay down my life for you. Jesus answered, Will you (really) lay down your life for Me? I assure you, most solemnly I tell you, before the rooster crows, you will deny me (completely disown me) three times. John 13:36-38 (AMP)

But we all know how long that commitment, and discipline lasted and how quickly it disappeared when a young girl who had seen him with Jesus confronted him.

4

If commitment, discipline and follow through were all that is needed to be a man of God then why would we need Jesus Christ as our Lord and Savior? All we would have to do is attend an Anthony Robins Personal Power Conference to be motivated. No, there is something much more powerful and deeper than mere commitment and follow-through, and that is the Love of God.

Peter did not want Jesus to die and go away. He was the disciple who said that he would stick with Jesus no matter what happened. Yet Jesus told him that he (Peter) would deny Him three times before the rooster crowed. And we all know that this truly happened. Three times Peter was accused of being one of Jesus disciples and three times, he denied it vehemently. And then as the rooster crowed, he looked up and saw Jesus looking at him. I can imagine the failure and disappointment he felt at his inability to stick to his word. How alone and lost he must have felt at having betrayed Jesus almost as badly as Judas did. He had come way short of his intention to stick with Jesus, even lay down his life for Him.

So often we do the same thing. We say we are never going to let Jesus go in every situation no matter what. Like the well-known song that we often sing: "Jesus, lover of my soul, Jesus, I will never let you go..." But when things go wrong and the mess happens, we do let go so quickly. We fail and fall short of our own hopes and expectations. What we actually need to do is take hold of the fact that Jesus never lets go of us! He knows that we are going to fall down and fail sometimes, but He never will let go.

Going fishing

Now Jesus had told the disciples to stay in Jerusalem to wait for the gift of the Holy Spirit who would help them go and fulfill the Great Commission. But after the crucifixion the disciples were at a lost as to what to do. I believe Peter felt he had failed in his personal discipline and commitment to Jesus so he decided to go fishing and the others agreed and went with him. John 21:3 "I go a fishing," and a whole bunch of them said, "We also go with you." I believe he felt that he was going to go back to what he (thought) he knew how to do which was fishing. The interesting thing is that every time we read about Peter and the disciples fishing, they never seem to catch anything. And Jesus had to help them out every time, but they were determined to go and try again anyway.

And this fishing trip was no different. They went out fishing and caught nothing all night long. Isn't this just how we are as human beings? When we feel we have failed, we decide that we will go back to what we think we can do, only to find out that we're not even able to do that successfully without God's help and intervention.

In the morning, the disciples saw a man who called out to them from the shore and told them to cast their nets on the right side of the boat, which they did and they made a huge catch. John realized it was Jesus on the shore talking to them and told Peter, who then jumped overboard and swam to the shore.

Our story picks up again after they have eaten and are sitting chatting.

Take off the Mask

Before we get into this subject, let's take a few moments to get honest with ourselves. Let's remove the masks we put on to give people around us a certain image of who we want them to think we are. Many of us are hurting but pretending that all is well so that others won't know how we really feel. We wear these masks around our Father (God) too, thinking that He doesn't really know who we are and we can hide our true feelings.

So put your hand on your chin, remove the mask and let's get studying.

Do You Love Me?

John 21:15-17 So when they had dined, Jesus saith to Simon Peter, Simon, son of Jonas, lovest thou me more than these? He saith unto him, Yea, Lord; thou knowest that I love thee. He saith unto him, Feed my lambs. He saith to him again the second time, Simon, son of Jonas, lovest thou me? He saith unto him, Yea, Lord; thou knowest that I love thee. He saith unto him, Feed my sheep. He saith unto him the third time, Simon, son of Jonas, lovest thou me? Peter was grieved because he said unto him the third time, Lovest thou me? And he said unto him, Lord, thou knowest all things; thou knowest that I love thee. Jesus saith unto him, feed my sheep. (KJV)

The Bible says that after this difficult time the disciples had gone through, Jesus affectionately says to Peter, "Peter, do you love me"? And we read that Peter said, "Yes Lord, you know that I love you." Jesus asks Peter a second time, "Peter, do you love me"? Again we read that Peter answers and says, "Yes Lord, you know that I love you"! Unfortunately when we just read this in the English language we do not get the true picture of what is being asked and what is being answered.

Unlike the English language the Greek language has several different words for expressing love. When we look at the different Greek words used here in this conversation between Jesus and Peter we find that it shines a whole new light on it. Something I certainly did not see immediately, even though I had read this scripture many times before.

When Jesus asked Peter if he loved him, He used the Greek word "Agapao" which is derived from the word "Agape" which is a very strong word for love. It actually speaks of the God kind of love; unconditional love, overwhelming love. In effect Jesus is asking Peter –

"Peter do you unconditionally, absolutely, overwhelmingly love me? Peter in return does not use the same word "Agapao" but instead uses the word "Phileo" which is a word used for friendliness, a brotherly love. Peter is actually saying "I like you Jesus, You're a nice guy."

Again the second time Jesus asks the same question and Peter gives the same answer. But the third time even though it appears that Jesus is again asking the same question, and that Peter is giving the same answer it is not so.

John 21:17 - He saith unto him the third time, Simon, son of Jonas, lovest thou me? Peter was grieved because he said unto him the third time, Lovest thou me? And he said unto him, Lord, thou knowest all things; thou knowest that I love thee. Jesus saith unto him, Feed my sheep. (KJV)

This time Jesus is not asking a question as much as He is questioning Peter's previous response or answers, because this time Jesus uses the word "Phileo" and not the word "Agapeo". Jesus is now actually questioning if Peter even liked Him. I believe that at this time in Peter's life, with all that had happened, his hopes being crushed, the perceived failure of his commitment and discipline, he was not even sure if he really liked Jesus or not. Jesus knew this and that is why he pressed this point with Peter. We can see that this was what was happening because the Bible says that Peter was grieved because the third time Jesus was questioning his commitment yet again, and the memory of the last time was still fresh in his mind.

Many of us fear this same question

On this trans-Atlantic flight, coming back from the USA I realized what this conversation was actually about. And the Lord spoke clearly to me saying that what He had asked Peter is the question Christians fear the most. This is the place where many, many Christians are today. So many of us are facing these same realities in our walk with God. Unfortunately many of us have learned to hide it or just fake it. We go around pretending that nothing is amiss and that we really love God. We even know how to turn on the tears and put on a good face when it comes to expressing it in praise and worship so that from the outside it looks like the real thing. But deep within us there is a real hunger to be deeply in love with God. We know that we should love God. We desperately want to love God, but it is just not there. Oh! We have fleeting moments and occasions where we experience true love, but they are all too soon gone and forgotten. So we become the great pretenders!

I believe many Christians, if they are really honest, cannot truly say that they love the Lord unconditionally and without reservation. It may sound harsh to say that but very often Christians cannot be honest with God or themselves. As long as you believe that God is angry with you or trying to trick you, you will never be honest with him.

A woman who is married to a hard and harsh man, who demands obedience regardless of what happens, cannot truly say that she loves him. She may obey him and do what is demanded, but can never really relax and enjoy his company. She can never be honest with her husband. Even to the point of going out, spending money and lying about it or hiding what she has bought. If you see God as harsh and judgmental, you can never be honest and open with Him. I have seen many people worshiping God and praising Him, but their hearts deny what they are doing. Many times we find it hard to really show love toward God.

However, Jesus knew Peter's heart. That's why he asked these questions. The Bible says that Peter was grieved that Jesus even asked whether he liked Him or not. If you are feeling this way and are not sure if you like Jesus, let me encourage you with this:

God (Jesus) is not concerned about whether you love Him or not. Wow, Arthur how can you say that?

I want to tell you something that the Lord shared with me that day on the airplane. This truth so impacted me that day I literally felt as if the bones in my body were shaking and quivering.

The Lord said to me, "Arthur, do you realize that I'm not really concerned if you love me or not? I almost fell out of my seat that day. I'm sure the lady next to me felt the tremors rushing through my body. This was such a shock to my religious system that at first I thought it was the devil speaking to me, but then I heard the Lord say, "It does not surprise me when you do not love me Arthur! I'm not taken back or shocked when I find out that you don't love me, but I am concerned and eager that you would know and believe that **I love you**."

This is exactly what John said in I John 4: 9-10, *Herein is love, not that we loved God, but that he loved us, and sent*

18

his Son to be the propitiation for our sins.
(KJV)

Surely we should love God!

True and many of us want to love Him but sometimes we just are not sure that we do. We need to realize that we need to respond to His love for us! God is more concerned about whether you know that HE loves YOU than that you love Him. God knows that you need to respond to His unconditional love. You cannot possibly give something you don't have. You cannot share a love that you have not experienced or accepted. The Bible gives no indication that Jesus had a nervous breakdown when Peter could not return the love He had shown. I don't believe God feels any differently. He doesn't get all bent out of shape when He realizes you don't love Him. He doesn't turn to Jesus and ask for His Prozac because He is unloved!

Now don't close the book and get all bent out of shape. Stay with me here and I will explain it all.

We have been told for many years that WE MUST love God in order to get anything from Him or to have the anointing flow through us or have Him love or bless us. We continually feel we need to love God more so that we can be blessed or have our children blessed. We have been told to "return to your first love" over and over again till we feel condemned and lost because we just don't know how. Returning to your first love is only coming back to the realization that YOU are loved by GOD. Come back to the One who loved you first. It is not something you do in order to get Him to love you again! His love for you has never changed and never will.

Chapter Two

Love is of God

John (who also wrote the book of I John) is known as the apostle of love, the one who put his head on Jesus' breast at the last supper. We are going to take time to look at some well-known verses in this letter he wrote.

I John 4:7-8 *Beloved, let us love one another for love is of God, and everyone that loveth is born of God and knoweth God. He that loveth not, knoweth not God.*

Unfortunately this scripture has caused much confusion in our lives. We think this means that we should go and love other people so that God can love us and that if we love others then that proves we love Him so that He can love us back. NO! This is what I call a dyslexic verse. A backwards verse. Basically all this verse states is that if you know God's love for you, then and only then will you be able to love others and when you love others it shows that you understand God's love for YOU! You can only share or give what you have received.

I John 4:9-10 *"In this was manifest the love of God toward us"*(This is how the love of God is shown toward us). *Herein is love* (this is what love is*), *not that we loved God ... but that He loved us and sent His son to be the propitiation for our sins...*

Mostly when the phrase "the love of God" is mentioned, people hear that they need to DO something or GO OUT and love others because this is what we have been taught. Note, this verse says the love of God is **"toward"** us. I am not talking about what you need to do but what God has done toward you! This is all about how He responds to YOU and not you to HIM!

My friend, please understand this, God is not concerned about whether you love Him or not. What is important to

God is: **Do you know that He loves you?** You can put on your mask and say the right things, but God sees your heart and knows what really goes on in it. Whether you love Him or not is not His greatest concern. He wants you to know that **HE LOVES YOU**! Once you realize His love for you, then loving Him is not a problem. Understanding His love for you is what brings peace and changes you!

Vs 16 ... *"we have known and believed the love that God has to us"*

You see, most Christians know and have heard about the love of God, but few BELIEVE it. It's easy to believe that He loved the world. But when it comes to us as individuals, we question whether we believe that or not. We know the promises we have made and failed to keep and the decisions we have made and not managed to maintain and we find it difficult to believe that He loves us in spite of that. We know how many times we have promised not to do certain things, but found ourselves doing the very things we said we would not do. We know how weak we are to keep a vow or promise that we have made to God. Our shortcomings and failures actually cause us to believe we are separated from the love of God.

This is my charge to you today. Don't just listen to what the love is about, but **believe** it. Start persuading your heart of His love toward you today. Don't wait a moment longer. Your very life depends on your understanding of this great love.

Paul makes an interesting statement in (Col 1:21) *"Once you were alienated from God and were enemies in your minds because of your evil behavior. (NIV)*

What we have done in the past (and many are still doing every day of their lives) is to alienate, separate or distance ourselves from God because we believe our failures somehow affect how God loves us. Notice where this alienation takes place; in your mind but not in God's mind. You are not God's enemy and He is not your enemy. It is failure to believe in His unconditional love for us that separates us in our own minds, causing much emotional pain and torment. He has never changed His mind toward us!

That is why John says that we must not only know but also believe (or be persuaded of) the love that God has to us.

Love the foundation.

The truth that most people seem to ignore is the fact that love is the foundation or essence for everything that God did. John 3:16 is a wonderful reminder of this. *"For God so LOVED the world that He gave His only begotten Son that whosoever believes in Him should not perish but have everlasting life."* (KJV) In I John 4:16 he also writes that **God is love;** *and he that dwelleth in love dwelleth in God, and God in him).*

God is love. Love is not something God does, love is who God is. Therefore no matter what God does it is Love doing it. It makes no difference how or when you come into contact with God, you will be contacting love. There is never a time when God is not love, when He will not love you, or cannot love you. Have you ever opened your Bible and found where God has changed His mind and said that He does not love the world and therefore takes back everything He has ever said and done for mankind? No! He is the same yesterday today and forever **(Heb 13:8).** In order for God not to love you He would have to cease to be God. He would have to stop existing!

The Measuring Stick

I John 4:17 *Herein is our love made perfect, that we may have boldness in the day of judgment: because as he is, so are we in this world.*

This is the only measuring stick for your life today. This is how you **know** that you have been perfected by the love of God or convinced about God's love for you. "In the day of judgment you will have boldness or confidence." I believe this means that you know God is not to blame any time you see or hear or even experience events or circumstances that look like it could be God's judgment on your life. This is true even when it seems like your prayers are not being answered, or things are just not working out for you like you planned. I believe it means that you would have such great boldness in God's love for you to know that it is not His judgment on your life, therefore being able to live free from dread or impending judgment. This means that even if hellfire and brimstone comes on the earth right now, you can stand boldly and state:

"This is not from God to me. It is a terrible thing, but it is not God's judgment on me."

How will I have boldness in the 'day of judgment'? *"Because as He is, so are you in this world"*

We are all in this world. We are not OF this world but we live IN it. We can have boldness in the 'day of judgment' - because **as He (Jesus) is, so are we in this world**.

- Where is Jesus today? He is seated at the right hand of God.

- Is God angry with Jesus right now? NO. As He is, so are we in this world right now!

If God is not angry with Jesus, then he is not angry with you!

- Is God upset with Jesus right now? NO. As He is, so are we in this world right now!

- Is God disappointed with Jesus right now? NO. As He is, so are we in this world right now!

- Is Jesus, sick, poor etc right now? NO. As He is, so are we in this world right now!

- Is God ashamed of Jesus? NO. As He is, so are we in this world right now!

If only we would believe these words! If the church would just believe one little part of this verse in the Bible, then things would be so different. God is not disappointed, ashamed, angry or anything else with you. As He is, so are you in this world. In order for God to be angry with you, He would have to be angry with Jesus.

There is No Fear in Love

I John 4:18: *There is no fear in love, but perfect love casts out fear because fear has torment*

Living Bible: " We need have no fear of someone who loves us perfectly; His perfect love for us eliminates all dread of what He might do to us. If we are afraid, it is for fear of what He might do to us, and shows that we are not fully convinced that He really loves us."

I like the way the Living Bible says this: *"We need have no fear of someone who loves us perfectly."* If there is anybody that is able to love perfectly it certainly must be God. Therefore we need not fear Him in any way, because if we do fear Him it shows that we do not really believe that He truly loves us.

So many people are afraid of God for so many different reasons and many are not serving God today because they fear His wrath and anger, instead of trusting in His unfailing, everlasting love. That is why so many Christians live in torment and emotional instability. Fear has torment. That word torment literally means dread, or an expectation of judgment.

The basis of our relationship with God is to be loved not our love for Him but His love for us. In (I Jn 4: 19) *"We love Him, because he first loved us."* No matter how you look at this, the love of God is the foundation for everything in the Bible, and the love of God is the beginning and end of everything concerning our Christian lives

If a man is not made perfect in love that means that he does not know and believe the love that God has for him or as Paul puts it, he does not know that he is "rooted and grounded in the love of God". No man can correctly interpret the Word of God without having his heart established in and upon the love of God.

I think it is important that we clarify what it means to be established in the love of God, or as some people would say 'walking in the love of God'.

The usual misunderstanding of walking in Gods love was clearly illustrated to me a few years ago. I was invited to one of the local churches in our city to hear a special guest speaker. The meeting was wonderful and I do not want anybody to think that what I want to say is in any way critical or condemning. In his message the guest speaker mentioned that while he was fasting and praying he asked the Lord to show him why the church is not experiencing the supernatural power of God like we see in the book of Acts. He said the Lord answered him and said, "It is because my people are not walking and living in my Love."

The speaker then went on to say that the reason the church is not experiencing the supernatural is because we are not walking in love towards one another in the body of Christ. Now although there is some truth in that, I do not believe that is what the Lord was saying at all. The man undoubtedly heard the voice of God, but interpreted it incorrectly.

Being established in the love of God or walking in the love of God is not being ABLE to love, but being able TO BE loved. It is about walking and living in the love that God has toward us first, and then and only then can we ever dream about loving others. If I walk in the spotlight on a stage, the light is not coming from me, but toward me. I am walking IN THE LIGHT. Just so when I walk in the love of God, it is not something coming from me but toward me.

Loving others can only be accomplished if we know and believe the love that God has to us, or as I like to put it, "Only when we will allow ourselves to be loved by God, are we starting to walk in His love."

This is the whole reason Jesus came - to show us the love of the Father. To show us that we are loved and that we can accept and receive His love for us. We have to remember that God's love for us does not depend on our performance.

John 3:16 *For God so* loved the world, *that he gave his only begotten Son, that whosoever believeth in him should not perish, but have everlasting life. (KJV)*

And in Romans Paul says it this way *"But God* demonstrates his own love for us *in this: While we were still sinners, Christ died for us."* (Rom 5:8) *(NIV)*

This is the awesome reality of the Gospel of Jesus Christ. The birth, life, death, resurrection and ascension of Jesus Christ is a spiritual, physical and emotional demonstration of God's love for mankind. It was a demonstration that was meant to convince all mankind of the love of God, and if it is correctly perceived then no man can ever doubt that God truly loves him. That means that no man has an excuse not to believe the love that God has for him.

Loved as He is loved

When Jesus prayed before His crucifixion, He said: *John 17: 22-26*

"I have given them the honor that You gave me, that they may be one, as we are one - I in them and you in me, that they may grow complete in one, so that the world may realize that You sent me and have loved them as You loved me. Father I want those whom You have given me to be with me where I am; I want them to see that glory which You have made mine - for You loved me before the world began."

"... I have made Your Self known to them and will continue so that the love which You have had for me may be in their hearts ...." J.B. Phillips

What a wonderful revelation Jesus gives us in this prayer. He says that He wants the world to know that God loves them, as He loves the Son, Jesus. Now how does the Father love the Son? When we read further Jesus goes on to say " *...for You have loved me before the world began."*

So if God loved Jesus before the world began, and Jesus wants us to know that God loves us as He loves Jesus, that means God also loved us before the world began. God's love for us started long before any sin, long before Adam committed high treason. We were created out of that love that He has for us. God did not stop loving us just because these things happened, for while we were yet sinners God demonstrated His love towards us and sent Jesus to die for the ungodly. The ungodly you might ask? Yes the ungodly, Jesus did not die for the righteous but for the ungodly. Those who did not even want anything to do with Him.

While we were yet in weakness [powerless to help ourselves], at the fitting time Christ died for (in behalf of) the ungodly. Now it is an extraordinary thing for one to give his life even for an upright man, though perhaps for a noble and lovable and generous benefactor someone might even dare to die. But God shows and clearly proves His [own] love for us by the fact that while we were still sinners, Christ (the Messiah, the Anointed One) died for us.
Rom 5:6-8

When you become convinced or persuaded in your heart that he loves you perfectly then you have no fear that He would do anything bad to you. The Bible does not say that you need not have fear of someone who loves you perfectly, **except when you sin**. There are no ifs, ands or buts. No conditions. Unfortunately religion always wants to put a "but" in there somewhere. There are no 'buts'. You are loved perfectly all the time.

This is not Greasy Grace

Many people say I preach a soft gospel, greasy grace or easy believe-ism. Let me ask you this question. How easy is it to believe that God loves you when you have just violated everything that you believe is right? Hebrews 4:16 tells us we should come boldly to the throne of grace where we will find grace and mercy to help in a time of need.

Let us then fearlessly and confidently and boldly draw near to the throne of grace (the throne of God's unmerited favor to us sinners), that we may receive mercy [for our failures] and find grace to help in good time for every need [appropriate help and well-timed help, coming just when we need it].

When is your time of need? When you have sinned! When you have missed it and you need help! But what do so many of us do when we fall, or sin or have a weak moment? We stay away from God for a couple of weeks trying to make up for it. How silly!

Remember I John 4:18 reminds us that His perfect love **eliminates** (casts out) all dread of what He will do to us. If you are afraid of what He may do, then it proves or shows that you are not fully convinced that He really loves you. Let your heart and mind believe this. All it takes is to believe so that any kind of fear that you may have will be eliminated. His love has already been shed abroad in your heart. It's already there – believe it! Start persuading your heart today!

You may be thinking: "Well I am not afraid of what God will do but maybe He has taken His hand of protection off me and when I do something wrong, the devil will have an inroad into my life to hurt me or kill me or do something to my family."

That's like me saying to my child, "Well I'm sorry, you didn't clean your room today so now you can just sleep outside on the steps." What would you do to someone who treats a child like that? Report them as child abusers!

Jesus said: "If you who are evil know how to take care of your children, how much more will your heavenly father take care of you?"

He Loved Us First

I John 4:19 - *"So you see our love for Him comes as a result of Him loving us first."*

Finally John comes to one conclusion and that is we can only respond with love to someone who loves US so unconditionally and unselfishly.

To further understand the power of this wonderful love of God, we need to go back to our story of Jesus and Peter in John 21. I believe the reason for recording the incident can actually be found in John 14:1. It is a story of hope and trust in the unfailing love of God.

After Jesus told Peter he would deny Him three times He went on to say: *"Do not let your hearts be troubled (distressed, agitated). You believe in and adhere to and trust in and rely on God; believe in and adhere to and trust in Me. In my Father's house are many dwelling places. If it were not so, I would have told you; for I am going away to prepare a place for you!"* John 14:1-2 (AMP)

This showed God's unconditional love! It didn't matter what Peter was going to do, Jesus still had his wellbeing in mind and declared hope and love from God toward Peter. He was still going to prepare a place for Peter even though Jesus knew Peter would fail.

What I want you to see is that you need to allow God to love you first in spite of what your life is like at the moment; in spite of your shortcomings. You don't understand the love of the Father if you think he doesn't love you. God doesn't care if you love him or not. If God could only love you when you are right and good, then His love is no better than that of a sinner. Jesus said: "If you love those who love you then you are no better than a sinner, for sinners love those who love them."

God loves you even though you can honestly say you don't love him or are not sure that you love him. I cried on that plane because for years I wasn't sure if I loved God or not. I was afraid if I said that then it would be over for me. God wouldn't want me anymore. I can remember I pulled down the shutter and hid in the dark, weeping. "God I really want to and desire to love you. I know I should love you, but I don't." And gently the Holy Spirit said: "It's ok, I love you anyway."

That day, I told the Lord that I would receive that love, even though I felt so inferior and unqualified. I decided I would let God love me in spite of it all. From that moment, the love of God became real and I experienced love like never before. And it hasn't stopped!

When I get to a place when I lose sight of the love of God for me, then all I do is find a quiet place, sit down and say: "Here I am Lord, love on me."

Getting Your Ducks In A Row

Unfortunately many people still want to get their ducks in a row first – let me stop smoking, let me stop drinking, stop beating my wife/children, let me first pray regularly, go to church every week, read my Bible every day etc before they allow God to love them in spite of themselves. The problem is that we can never get our ducks in a row, so we spend every day just getting further and further away from God's love. And then we wonder why we cant love other people.

I was in ministry for eight years and I hated people. I was a pastor and felt like bashing people's heads in because I was so unhappy. I was in a terrible place of insecurity and blamed other people for how I felt. I believe many ministers feel the same way but won't admit it. Just listen to some of their preaching. They preach a bunch of angry messages because they believe they serve an angry God. You become like the God you serve or you believe He is. If you believe God is judgmental, then you become like that too.

What Does It Mean When God Says He Loves You?

Now, it's easy for me to say: "Let God love you", but many of us don't even know what that means. How does true unconditional love behave? Our perspective has been so perverted that we don't know what true love is. A man will beat up a woman and then say: "I do that because I love you. I want you to be a better person". Our understanding of true love has become so warped by the world's view of things that we think God behaves the same way. We equate love with hurt and think that is what God is going to do to us too. So many people who have hurt us, say they love us so we project that onto God and expect the same treatment from Him.

I want you not only to **know or understand** the love of God, but also to **experience** it and become convinced in your heart that there is a certain way God will treat you when he says he loves you. We will look at that next.

Discover True Love

Chapter Three

A Biblical Definition of God's Love

I Corinthians 13 is a declaration of the wonderful view of God's love and what to expect when we know and understand that love.

If I (can) speak in the tongues of men and (even) of angels, but have not love I am only a noisy gong or a clanging cymbal. And if I have prophetic powers (the gift of interpreting the divine will and purpose), and understand all the secret truths and mysteries and possess all knowledge, and if I have [sufficient] faith so that I can remove mountains, but have not love (God's love in me) I am nothing (a useless nobody). Even if I dole out all that I have [to the poor in providing] food, and if I surrender my body to be burned or in order that I may glory, but have not love (God's love in me), I gain nothing.

Even if you can speak in other languages, prophecy and give to the poor, it means absolutely nothing without understanding the love God has FOR YOU. All you will be is a tinkling cymbal or sound of dull brass. There is a lot of noise in the church today that doesn't mean much because people don't really understand God's unconditional love.

Most of what we have heard preached from this passage of scripture is how we should behave. How we should treat others. I want to show you a different way to look at it.

I have spent a good portion of this book showing you that God is love (1 John 4:8, and 1 John 4:16). The word "is" is a mathematical equation i.e. God equals or is equal to (=) love. If God is love it stands to reason that love is God. God cannot be separated from his love therefore love is who God is, and not something God does. God cannot give His love away like I would give my wallet to my wife. Now if God is love then it is not something that God can turn on and off at will. It is not separate from Him. It is WHO HE IS.

The significance of this is that, in order for God not to love, He would have to cease to be God and we all know that's never going to happen. If God is not going to cease to be God that means God will never not love us.

So if God is love and love is God, then when we read the word love in the next few verses it is really also talking about what love is like. When God says he loves us this is what we can expect from Him toward us. Remember it's **His love toward us**.

God Is Love

Love endures long and is patient and kind; love never is envious nor boils over with jealousy, is not boastful or vainglorious, does not display itself haughtily.

Love (God) endures long and is patient and kind. When God says He loves you, He endures long and is patient and kind. God is not impatient. Love never is envious or boils over with jealousy.

When we read this verse from the perspective of God's love towards us, it means that when God says that He loves us, He endures long and is patient and kind with us under all circumstances.

It means that God will always be

long suffering and patient with us in all of our endeavors of life.

I am the type of person who can easily get discouraged by my own shortcomings, inabilities and weaknesses. Especially when I find that I'm not learning as fast as many others around me. All my life I've been a slow learner and for most of my life I have had to pay dearly for not keeping up with my peers either in school, college or just in life in general. As a result I become frustrated and impatient with myself and more often than not I will seem to think that God must feel the same way about me as I'm feeling about myself, but this cannot be further from the truth.

In Matthew 11: 29, Jesus teaching his disciples what it is like to know God and to be intimate with God says, *"Take the burden of responsibility I give you and thereby discover your life and your destiny. I am gentle and humble; I am willing to relate to you and to permit you to learn at your own rate; then in fellowship with me, you will discover the meaning of your life."* [Ben Campbell Johnson – paraphrase]

You can imagine how wonderful it was for me to learn that God, the Almighty, the creator of the universe says that He is willing to relate to me and what is more overwhelming is that He will allow me to learn at my own rate. When God says that He loves me he will be patient, and kind to me letting me learn at my own rate and the same is true of you! What wonderful freedom and rest there is in knowing the love of God toward us.

Are you convinced by now that God loves you? Then you know He is not envious or boils over with jealousy. True, the Bible does talk about God being a jealous God, but this is not the green monster of jealousy because He doesn't want you to have fun in life. He is not jealous of what you do but He is jealous because He wants you for Himself. He is jealous in the sense that He sent Jesus so He could make sure that you would enjoy relationship with Him.

However, God is not jealous if you have a hobby that doesn't include church activities, the Bible or Bible studies etc. So many people live totally driven by their Christianity. They had other interests before but since becoming believers they just feel uncomfortable doing those things or think they are wrong now.

My Fun Story

I always loved playing golf but for 9 or 10 years in ministry I could not go out and enjoy a good game. When I got to the golf course I would feel guilty because I thought I could rather be praying or visiting the sick or studying or whatever other church activities there were. I didn't really think God wanted me to have fun because He was jealous of my life and other interests I had.

At first I thought I had solved my problem by taking my Walkman with me so I could listen to a tape while playing golf (that's what we used back in the day). Now, those of you who know the game understand that golf is difficult enough without having some Bible teacher talking in your ear at the same time. Just the sound of the blood rushing through your ears is enough to disturb your concentration! So many ministers/pastors admit they play golf (for instance), but qualify their actions by saying: "But I was listening to so and so while playing", or "I was praying in the Spirit", as if that makes it all ok. All they are doing is trying to soothe their own consciences or the sense that they feel God is condemning them.

Relax!! God wants you to enjoy life because He enjoys you enjoying what He has blessed you with!

It (God or love) is not conceited (arrogant and inflated with pride); it is not rude (unmannerly) and does not act unbecomingly. Love (God's love in us) does not insist on its own rights or its own way, for it is not self-seeking;

When God says He loves you He will not be rude to you or arrogant or act unbecomingly. He is not inflated with pride. Why do you allow pastors, evangelists and other men or women of God to preach to you and be rude while doing so? Why do we allow them to behave badly and then excuse it by saying: "Wow they really trod on our toes today and straightened us up". NO!! If God says He wont behave like that, then we shouldn't allow other people to talk to us like that either.

Love (God) does not insist on His own rights or His own way. God will direct you but never insist on everything His way. Does God have rights? Does God have

His own way? Yes He does, but if we understand His love for us we will know that He does not insist on it, in and for our lives but gently directs our paths.

Deut 30:19 *I call heaven and earth to record this day against you, that I have set before you life and death, blessing and cursing: therefore choose life, that both thou and thy seed may live: (KJV)*

God's way is life and blessing, but he says: "I put before you life and death, blessing and cursing but I will not insist on you taking life! But please choose life and blessing". All this means is that God loves us so much that He will leave the life choices up to us and He will love us in and through it all. If we succeed He loves us and if we fail He loves us, this takes all the fear out if living life to the full and enjoying it. He leaves the choice up to you and loves you and blesses, heals and prospers you all the way even if you make a wrong decision.

In the church we have a teaching concerning the perfect or permissive will of God where believers are taught that God allows certain things to happen to them to teach them something. NO! That isn't true either. God never allows stuff to happen to us. He always wants the best and loves us no matter what. God is the one who is always there to help pick up the pieces when we need Him. He's the one who will warn you and help you along the road of life. He is the one who is always on hand to pick you up and help.

Believing that God allows or causes the pain in your life is like me saying that I know who causes accidents on our roads. I believe it's the police and the paramedics who cause accidents. After all whenever I see an accident, the police and paramedics are there, so they must be the cause of the accidents. Ridiculous thought isn't it? Well that's how silly it is to say that God causes or allows 'accidents' in our lives! He isn't there because He caused the problem. NO! He is there to HELP you out of the situation. HE IS THE HELP.

... it (love or God) is not touchy or fretful or resentful; it takes no account of the evil done to it [it pays no attention to a suffered wrong].

God (love) isn't touchy or fretful either. I always thought that when I don't do what He wants, He throws a fit and gets all touchy about it. When we make mistakes, God doesn't go to Jesus and say: "I just can't believe what happened. Jesus, did you see what Arthur did?" God doesn't fall off His throne when you make a mistake. Psalm 103 tells us: "I know your frame. I know what you are made of. You are made of dust. Basically God says: "I know you are a dirt bag" (my joking paraphrase).

God (love) takes no account of evil done to it (him). You can be assured that when you do anything that directly opposes Him, He doesn't keep a record of it. He doesn't say: "Bring me that record-keeping book. I want to record this matter against Arthur." He pays no attention to a suffered wrong.

It does not rejoice at injustice and unrighteousness, but rejoices when right and truth prevail.

Who Believes In You?

Love (God) bears up under anything and everything that comes, is ever ready to believe the best of every person, its hopes are fadeless under all circumstances, and it endures everything [without weakening].

No matter what happens or how bad or big a situation is God (love) is ever ready to believe the best. There is an advertisement about "Eveready" batteries in a toy Easter bunny and how they keep on keeping on. Well God (love) is like that. Always ready to believe the best no matter how small that best may be. If there is only 10% best in you, then God believes in that.

Sometimes there are things that happen in our lives that make us feel like it is the end of the world. For many people death in a family, or divorce is so devastating that they feel like it is the end of their lives or even the end of their ministry. But the love of God for us is able to bear up under anything and everything that comes. Divorce, mistakes, bankruptcy, people spreading lies about you, pretty much anything destructive, does not have to mean the end of your life or if you're a minister it does not have to be the end of your ministry. It is true our lives might not be exactly the way it was before but God can restore us. With God it is never over because when he says He loves us he *is ever ready to believe the best of every person, its hopes are fadeless under all circumstances, and it endures everything [without weakening]."*

It's not who YOU believe in that makes a difference in your life. It's who believes IN YOU that makes that wonderful difference. It doesn't matter who declares your faults to God - He doesn't care. He continues to believe only the best.

Love never fails [never fades out or becomes obsolete or comes to an end].

God (love) NEVER, EVER FAILS. It never comes to an end. God just gets "gooder" and "gooder" as one person told me. There will never be a time when God (love) decides He has had enough of mankind. This message makes me happier and happier every time I preach it.

What an amazing love the Father has for us, yet we find it so difficult to believe. But believing this truth is the most important aspect of our Christian lives. Without this truth firmly rooted and grounded in our hearts there is no foundation for our faith. We have no reason to trust God and we have no reason to hope or have a confident expectation of good things.

Faith, Hope and Love

At the end of this great love chapter in Corinthians 13 Paul tells us that there are three ingredients that are essential for Christian life.

And now these three remain: faith, hope and love. But the greatest of these is love. Pursue and seek to acquire (this) love (make it your aim, your great quest).
1 Corinthians 13:13-14 *(NIV)*

Faith, Hope and Love, is the atmosphere in which God operates. Paul says that faith, hope and love are the three most important things we need in our Christian lives. Faith sees and believes the answer or the solution before it comes. Hope is a confident expectation of good things, so hope always expects what faith sees and believes. And the love of God is the ingredient that guarantees it.

This is why I firmly believe that at every opportunity I preach and teach the word of God I must always seek to establish people in faith, hope and love.

74

And if I do not have the time to teach them all three I will do my best to establish them on the love of God. For Paul says " But the greatest of these is Love. " Love has the ability to lead people into faith and hope.

Do you remember the account of Jairus, the ruler of the synagogue, who came to Jesus desiring Him to heal his daughter?

While he yet spake, there came from the ruler of the synagogue's house certain which said, Thy daughter is dead: why troublest thou the Master any further? As soon as Jesus heard the word that was spoken, he saith unto the ruler of the synagogue, Be not afraid, only believe. And he suffered no man to follow him, save Peter, and James, and John the brother of James. And he cometh to the house of the ruler of the synagogue, and seeth the tumult, and them that wept and wailed greatly. And when he was come in, he saith unto them, Why make ye this ado, and weep? the damsel is not dead, but sleepeth. And they laughed him to scorn. But when he had put them all out, he taketh the father and the mother of the damsel, and them that were with him, and entereth in where the damsel was lying. And he took the damsel by the hand, and said unto her, Talitha cumi; which is, being interpreted, Damsel, I say unto thee, arise. And straightway the damsel arose, and walked; for she was of the age of twelve years. And they were astonished with a great astonishment. Mark 5:35-42 (KJV)

This poor man gets Jesus to come with him and on the way to his house there are a couple of unexpected stops and eventually the message comes that his daughter has already died. He hears the words: *"Why troublest thou the Master any further?"* His heart sinks in his chest probably thinking: "Yes who am I? After all if it was Gods will to heal my daughter then this other woman with the issue of blood would not have delayed us so long." Maybe he thought that the woman with the issue got the healing that his daughter needed. But whatever it was, Jesus (who was the full expression of the love of God) soon rectified it by saying *"be not afraid, only believe "* Jesus just kept this man in a state of faith and hope. Jesus Himself (love) guaranteed the answer to the man's faith and hope.

It might be that today you are thinking along the same lines as this man did. "Why am I troubling the Master any further?" Sometimes we think that the problem we have is not important enough to warrant Gods personal attention. No, no, my friend! God is love and love endures long and is patient. That means that God will never give up on you. He will stick with it to the end.

No matter what your problem is, God is not going to ignore you because He is doing his own thing. His Love will always attend to you first. **For Gods Love is not self-seeking. It takes no account of evil done to it; Gods love pays no attention to a suffered wrong.** We need not fear that we are going to inconvenience Him with any of our problems or with our prayers.

You see if you have the love of God on your side, or if your heart is established in God's love for you, His love will always lead you into faith and hope.

Jesus just continued on to the man's house and even tried to lead the others at the house into faith and hope but they just laughed Him to scorn. He put them out because He could only work in an environment of Faith, Hope and Love. He took the damsel by the hand and said, "Arise!" and she came back to life again.

Being established in and on the love of God is absolutely essential for living a healthy Christian life.

The Message Bible: *Go after a life of love as if your life depended on it – because it does! (I Corinthians 14:1)*

This is Too Good to be True

You may be thinking that you are not too sure if you can believe this message. Perhaps you think it's too easy. Then I want to tell you that even if you just WANT to believe it, it's already enough. Will you take the first step and allow God to love you just as you are, right now? That's all you need to do for now. Maybe you feel like Peter, that you just can't say you truly love God without reservation. When you make that decision to allow God to love you unconditionally, as you are, then the reality of that love starts to take root in your heart.

Believe me, my friend, when you realize the love God has for YOU, you can never stand aside and not love Him back.

It is a natural response to love the person who loves you.

Chapter Four

God Speaks a Language of Love

Now many of us have heard teaching about hearing the voice of God and perhaps its one of the first things we learn as Christians. We hear that the voice of God can come through prophecy, studying the word, perhaps through a preacher etc. While these are all true ways to hear the voice of God, one of the primary ways God speaks is in that still, small voice within us. Have you ever heard someone say: "Something told me this or that"? Sometimes it's not quite a "voice", but a knowing that God is saying something in your heart or that you just know that you know.

However, there have been times in the past that I felt the Lord speaking to me but was just unable to define exactly WHAT He was saying.

What I want to look at here is not the fact that God speaks, or how He speaks, but how to know or hear WHAT He has to say, when He does speak. We read of several instances in the Bible where God spoke and I feel that we can learn from these times, especially in the life of Jesus. Often when God spoke around Jesus, the people "heard" something, but were not always aware that it was God speaking. They often thought it was an angel or a thundering noise. We are all the same. We often misinterpret what someone says or don't always understand what is said.

John 10:1-5 (KJV) *Verily, verily, I say unto you, He that entereth not by the door into the sheepfold, but climbeth up some other way, the same is a thief and a robber. But he that entereth in by the door is the shepherd of the sheep. To him the porter openeth; and the sheep hear his voice: and he calleth his own sheep by name, and leadeth them out. And when he putteth forth his own sheep, he goeth before them, and the sheep follow him: for they know his voice. And a stranger will they not follow, but will flee from him: for they know not the voice of strangers.*

Note here that Jesus says:

1. The sheep HEAR the shepherd's voice
2. The sheep KNOW the shepherd's voice

God is constantly speaking and teaching but many of us have not been able to hear or understand Him. We have been lead to believe that only special people can hear the voice of God, and that we need these special people to speak into our lives and give us the Word of the Lord.

There is an erroneous teaching in the church today that causes believers to forsake their own intimate relationship with God in order to have someone else prophesy over them on an ongoing basis. I'm not discounting the fact that people do flow in the gift of prophesy and hear from God, but one of the greatest privileges we believers have is that we can hear the voice of God ourselves. We have been given the access and privilege of communing with God the Father. No more do we need an intermediary between God and us. *Jesus taught that we would also hear the voice of God.*

It's all very well to hear the voice, but it is another thing entirely to know what that voice is saying.

The Heart Condition of Man

Now when I say we can't always understand what God says I don't mean that I think God speaks badly or that He has some sort of a speech impediment. I do believe however that there is a condition in our hearts that determines how and what we hear from God, even when we hear the word of God preached.

If a man or a woman is not established in their hearts (or belief system) in the love, kindness and the goodness of God, they cannot correctly interpret the word of God.

If your heart is not established, or fully persuaded of God's love and kindness toward YOU, the chances are good that you will always misinterpret what He is saying when He speaks or when you read the Bible. This happens even though you may be able to understand the language it was said or written in.

This is also true of hearing the voice of God. I have often had people listen to me preach and then talk to me afterwards and completely misquote or misinterpret what I said. Again, this is not because they do not understand my accent or language, but because of what they believe in their hearts. Hearing what someone has to say has as much to do with the hearer as the speaker. The ability to understand correctly and comprehend what is being communicated has to do with the person's belief system. What they believe about God, about themselves, about others and their circumstances or situation has a great influence on how or what they hear.

This Love Cannot Be Exaggerated

Rom 8:31-9:1 *What then shall we say to these things? If God is for us, who can be against us?* If God is for you who in the world can be against you? This awesome GOD is FOR you!

The Hubble telescope has taken amazing pictures of galaxies being "born". One of the clouds they have photographed looks like a hand and has a "finger" that is 30 billion light years long. The awesome God who created this, is FOR you. So many times we read the Bible or listen to a message for someone else. But the fact is that God has done everything for YOU. Believe it! Make it personal because God is a personal God.

*He who did not spare His own Son,
but delivered Him up for us all, how shall He
not with Him also freely give us all things?*
God gives us ALL things FREELY. The
Good News of Jesus Christ is FREE. If
you want to pay for it or do anything to
get it, you can't have it. You can only
have it freely.

*Who can lay a charge against you?
Not God, He is the one who justifies you. Who
shall bring a charge against God's elect? It is
God who justifies.* God will never bring a
charge against you because He is the one
who justifies you!

*Who is he who condemns? It is Christ
who died, and furthermore is also risen, who is
even at the right hand of God, who also makes
intercession for us.* Who can condemn
you? Christ? No, He is the one who died

and was resurrected FOR you. He is at the right hand of the Father interceding FOR you. When you make a mistake or mess up, He declares you righteous because of what HE has done.

Who shall separate us from the love of Christ? Shall tribulation, or distress, or persecution, or famine, or nakedness, or peril, or sword? For I am persuaded that neither death nor life, nor angels nor principalities nor powers, nor things present nor things to come, nor height nor depth, nor any other created thing, shall be able to separate us from the love of God which is in Christ Jesus our Lord. (NKJV)

Who can separate you from the love of Christ? No one and nothing can! We need to become persuaded that nothing can separate us from the love of

God in Christ. "But Arthur, you don't know my life and what I have done." No, my friend, you don't know our God and His love for you. The Bible tells us that while we were sinners Christ died for us. *Rom 5:8 But God commends his love toward us, in that, while we were yet sinners, Christ died for us (KJV)*

We did nothing to deserve any of it, yet He did it anyway. If He died for us when we were sinners what makes us think that we can be removed from this incredible love when we make mistakes or sin now?

If you are not fully persuaded of your righteousness and standing in love, you will not be able to hear the voice of God clearly or learn to understand what He says.

Heart Conditions

Ephesians 3:14-17 *For this cause I bow my knees unto the Father of our Lord Jesus Christ, Of whom the whole family in heaven and earth is named, That he would grant you, according to the riches of his glory, to be strengthened with might by his Spirit in the inner man; That Christ may dwell in your hearts by faith;*

To hear WHAT God is saying and to interpret it has to do with the condition of your heart, that is, what you **believe.** The first thing that needs to happen in order to hear the voice of God is,

You must be a believer

You must know Jesus as your Lord and Savior and He must dwell in your heart by faith. There are people who believe that they are Christians simply because they were born in a so-called Christian country. Often when I tell people that the Lord spoke to me, they answer with, "You mean God actually speaks to you?" Their next response is often, "Do you answer Him?" They just don't understand that as a believer you can hear God speak to you. You must believe that what Jesus has done for you is a finished (completed) work and that through this work, you are declared righteous. You are a new person (creation).

2 Cor 5:17 *Therefore if any man be in Christ, he is a new creature: old things are passed away; behold, all things are become new. (KJV)*

The second thing is that you must realize **you are rooted and grounded in the love of God.**

*Ephesians 3:17 b: "that ye, **being** rooted and grounded in love,*

Note this is something that is already done. It says "being" rooted and grounded. It is something that is already done. It's not something you need to make happen. How is this possible that you are already rooted and grounded? The Bible tells us that God is love. It also tells us that we are in His hand. If we are in His hand, then we are in love. And nothing can pluck us out of His hand, so **nothing** can pluck us out of His love. The book of Romans tells us that we already have the love of God shed abroad in our hearts. Unfortunately there are many

Christians who don't know or believe this fact.

What does it mean to be rooted and grounded in this love? We need to become fully persuaded in your heart and mind that **nothing at all** can ever separate us from the love of God that is in Christ Jesus. No person, no circumstance, no situation, no devil, nothing at all can separate me from the love of God!

Comprehend this Love

Paul continues to say, Eph 3:*18 May be able to comprehend with all saints what is the breadth, and length, and depth, and height;*

From the Vine's Expository Dictionary, the word comprehend means **to lay hold of so as to possess as one's own,** hence it has the same two-fold meaning as the English word: **to apprehend, to seize upon, to take possession of, with beneficial effect.**

This means that if you want to comprehend, lay hold of, possess as your own, take possession of everything God has for you (something good), you need to realize you are rooted in the love of God. You need to established and persuaded that nothing can separate you from that love. This way you become aware of the length, breadth, height and depth of this love.

Eph 3:19 *And to know the love of Christ, which passeth knowledge, that ye might be filled with all the fullness of God."*

The Amplified reads: *That you may really come] to know [practically, through experience for yourselves] the love of Christ, which far surpasses mere knowledge [without experience]; that you may be filled [through all your being] unto all the fullness of God [may have the richest measure of the divine Presence, and become a body wholly filled and flooded with God Himself]!*

Many people have said that I exaggerate the love of God and put too much emphasis on it, but according to this statement, I can never over-emphasize the love of God. Because it passes mere knowledge that man has. The love of God goes beyond my imagination or what I can dream up about what I think it is.

We need to be in this love or realize we are in this love in order to seize upon and possess for ourselves what God is saying through His word and His Spirit. The problem I see in the Body of Christ is that we have never learned to understand the Language of this Love.

Unfortunately we have learned the Language of Law instead.

Discover True Love

Chapter Five

What is This Language of Love?

Just being born and living on this planet makes you a good candidate for the Language of Law. It is deeply engraved in our very nature. Every institution we have in society, our schools, political systems etc amplifies or re-enforces the law and legalism. Our everyday lives also speak about this law. For instance as parents we reward our children when they are good and we spank or discipline them when they are bad. If you work hard and apply yourself, you get a promotion. If you don't work hard, you get passed over. If you work hard at school and get good grades, you do well and you qualify for a good job. If not, you fail. We grow up believing all of life is like this. Even in the church we have used this means to promote or place people in places of importance or position. Faithfulness is good but because of our law upbringing we have come to believe that we only get what we deserve in life. With God you don't get what you deserve, you get what He has because of His mercy. Your efforts and good works do not qualify you.   Only Jesus qualifies you for everything God has provided.

Colossians 1:12 *Giving thanks for the Father, Who has qualified us and made us fit to share the portion which is the inheritance of the saints in the Light.* This type of thinking goes so completely against modern day thought.

Because we are under the law we are well versed in this way of law thinking. So when we come to God we treat him on the same level. We understand this language of law so that when we come to God we also expect him to speak to us in this language. We expect Him to speak a language of discipline and don't expect Him to do anything unless we do our part first. It has been preached like this and we think this is what it means because of our heart belief.

We think that if we DO something then God will move, but He says that if we want what He has, it only comes free, no payment needed. We don't understand His love language because we are waiting for it to be a language of law, based on what we already believe.

Rom 3:19-20 *Now we know that what things soever the law saith, it saith to them who are under the law...*

The law speaks to those who live under that law. If you always hear about and are conscious of your failures, mistakes and inabilities, then you are living under the law. What is the law? Not only the 10 commandments.

Anything you think you must do in order to please God or do for God to be acceptable is law. It may be prayer time, reading the Bible, or attending church, things you think give you favor with God and 'score points' with Him. Prayer, Bible reading, or correct behavior etc should be a response to who God is, not something you do to be his favorite.

If you think that you have to do things to impress God, the law will cause your mouth to be stopped because you know you cant do it anyway. This is what the law is designed to do. ... *that every mouth may be stopped, and all the world may become guilty before God. (Rom 3:19)*

How many times have you desired to spend time with God and fellowship with him? You make time to get up early but find that it is hard to communicate, or you fall asleep or there is always something else that gets in the way. Something else you find you would rather do. And when you fail to keep this law you have set for yourself, you feel unqualified and that you need to make up for lost time or reading or whatever. It can become a vicious cycle when it gets out of hand and eventually you find yourself giving up on it altogether. You find it hard to pray. It feels as if your mouth is stopped and you feel unqualified. That is a sure indication that you are living under the law.

The Responsibility Of The Law

Imagine driving down a highway merrily minding your own business when all of a sudden a traffic officer waves you over. So as a good Christian you pull over and wait for him to approach your car on the driver's side, in your rear view mirror you see that he has a book in his hands and as he is approaching your car he is writing down your car registration number. He finally gets to your window and greets you with a big smile, "Good morning, could I see your drivers license please". As you are taking out your wallet you say, "Is there a problem officer"? "No, not at all!" he says, "I am going to give you a commendation for $500."

"A commendation you exclaim!" "Yes," he says, "because you are such a good driver. You keep the speed limit, you are courteous, and you are a good example". "This commendation can be handed in at the local county court and they will give you $500".

Wouldn't that be a wonderful experience? I am sure that this has never happened to you. Right? In fact this has never happened to any one I have ever met or spoken to, because it is not the purpose of the law to issue commendations.

It is the law's responsibility to point out your failure to keep the speed limit, and the rules of the road and warn you when you are not courteous. Just as sure as a traffic officer would not give you a commendation, just so the voice of the Law will never mention your **improvements** or **acknowledge** your efforts.

The Language of Law Never Changes

The language of the law is always the same. It never changes. It is designed to point out every flaw, failure and mistake you ever make. God created the law to communicate your failures and to show your inabilities so you would turn to grace. The law questions every action and examines every motive. The law will never acknowledge that you tried. It just says, "You failed!" "Yes but I tried so hard", you say. But it doesn't care. It is just designed to point out the fault.

The work of the law makes you guilty. If you want to live under it, you will always feel rotten, guilty, condemned and unaccepted. The longer we live under the law, the less you will want to fellowship with the Lord. If you are living under the law you will always be conscious of your failure, inabilities and the fact that you are not good enough. The law was not given for us to live by. It was given so that we could see our inability to live by it. That is why we need the mercy of God.

This does not mean the law is evil. In fact the law is good. I believe the law is a revelation of the nature of God. The 10 commandments are the character of God, revealing who He is. And when his holiness and righteousness is revealed, it will shine light on our inabilities aside from God. It is the law's very nature to do this. Paul says the law is good and righteous, designed to bring you to the realization that you cannot do it.

So this is often where we stand when we want to fellowship with the Lord. We expect God to address our failures, to tell us that we need to shape up and change before we can stand in his presence. It's as if we feel we have failed or messed up and we expect something bad to happen because of the law we live under. Then, when things do happen to go wrong in our lives, we feel as if we have "paid" for our mistakes. But this is not true. Jesus paid for our sin and mistakes.

Rom 3:20 *Therefore by the deeds of the law there shall no flesh be justified in his sight: for by the law is the knowledge of sin. KJV*

We cannot be justified by the works of our flesh, or keeping the law because the law only brings the knowledge of sin or our inabilities and will keep pointing out those things as long as we use it as a guide in our lives.

Stick with me now! It gets better as we go along!

Chapter Six

Learning the Language of Love

Our biggest problem is that when we expect God to speak a language of law and correction but He speaks a language of love, we find we cannot understand him and get frustrated with our Christian life. Many of us are missing out on an intimate relationship and fellowship with our Father because we are not able to hear His words of LOVE.

In South Africa most people can speak and understand at least two languages. I speak and understand English and Afrikaans, which is a language similar to Dutch. Many times I have gone into a store expecting to hear English. My brain and mind are ready to process this English language and then suddenly the sales person will speak Afrikaans. Boy does that mix me up for a while! For the first few seconds I have no clue what they are saying. I have to ask them to repeat it because I was expecting one sound and got another.

This is what happens when we expect God to speak a language of law. We expect Him to correct, show our failures and flaws, but he speaks in love instead. We hear him speaking but have no idea what He is saying. Then because we don't understand, we think there must be some hidden meaning in what is happening. We decide that God must have told us in a nice way that we are scoundrels instead of just saying it out loud as it is. I would venture to say that 99% of the time we misinterpret because we are not expecting the language of love.

Here is a perfect example in the Bible about hearing the voice of God. I am going to take some license to illustrate this story. (This is just humor and my effort at making the story a bit more realistic).

Matt 16:5-12 *And when his disciples were come to the other side, they had forgotten*

to take bread. Then Jesus said unto them, Take
heed and beware of the leaven of the Pharisees
and of the Sadducees. And they reasoned
among themselves, saying, It is because we
have taken no bread. Which when Jesus
perceived, he said unto them O ye of little
faith, why reason ye among yourselves,
because ye have brought no bread? Do ye not
yet understand, neither remember the five
loaves of the five thousand, and how many
baskets ye took up? Neither the seven loaves of
the four thousand, and how many baskets ye
took up? How is it that ye do not understand
that I spake it not to you concerning bread,
that ye should beware of the leaven of the
Pharisees and of the Sadducees? Then
understood they how that he bade them not
beware of the leaven of bread, but of the
doctrine of the Pharisees and of the Sadducees.

116

When Jesus and the disciples got to the other side, they found that they had made a mistake and forgotten to take bread with them. Maybe it was Judas, the keeper of the moneybag who realized what they had done. He goes to Peter and says, "We forgot to bring bread! Who was responsible for this?" And Peter says: "I don't know. It must have been John or Matthew or …." Strange how it is when things go wrong that suddenly no one wants to take responsibility. But no matter who was at fault, the Bible says THEY had forgotten to take the bread.

My guess is that Peter says to them, "Whatever you all do, please don't tell Jesus. He has enough to worry about without thinking about stuff like this. We made this mistake, we will fix it." Peter, being the son of thunder, is probably wondering who it could be so that he can get them for it.

Just then (doubting) Thomas pops up in the scene. "Hey guys, what's happening? What's all the fuss about?" Peter tells him. "Well," Thomas says," I knew this was going to happen. I doubt Jesus will do another miracle. He's already done two miracles to feed people and we forgot to take bread both those times too." The disciples were totally perplexed by the situation.

Just at this point in the confusion, Jesus enters the scene and says, *"Take heed and beware of the leaven of the Pharisees and of the Sadducees."*

I can just imagine what happens. Peter says, "I just don't know how he does this! How does he know? We never get away with anything. I don't understand this at all. All we had to do is remember bread? How difficult is that? Now Jesus knows and I'm all embarrassed!"

The Bible says, *"And they reasoned among themselves, saying, "It is because we have taken no bread."*

Jesus realized what they were thinking and said: *"O ye of little faith, why reason ye among yourselves, because ye have brought no bread? Do ye not yet understand, neither remember the five loaves of the five thousand, and how many baskets ye took up? Neither the seven loaves of the four thousand and how many baskets ye took up? How is it that ye do not understand that I spoke it not to you concerning bread that ye should beware of*

*the leaven of the Pharisees and of the
Sadducees? Then understood they how that he
bade them not beware of the leaven of bread,
but of the doctrine of the Pharisees and of the
Sadducees. KJV*

You see, they were expecting Jesus
to confront their mistake or failure or
inability. Jesus was trying to give them a
life lesson but they were so focused and
conscious of their failure that they
misunderstood what he said and assumed
that He was addressing their failure.

We are no different. If we become
so focused and aware of our failures and
inabilities all the time, it becomes almost
impossible to correctly hear what God is
saying through His word. A man who is
continually aware of his failures and

shortcomings will always misinterpret the word when he reads it.

It is time to realize that Jesus has come to show you a better way to hear the Father. It is time to let go of the reasoning that thinks God is out to confront your mistakes, failures and inabilities. Whatever it is that you think you did that God can't forgive, put it behind you now and accept that He only wants you to realize His absolute passion and love for you.

If you want to hear what God is saying to you, keep your heart established on his love and caring for you.

Discover True Love

Chapter Seven

That We Might Have Life

John 8:1-11 is a wonderful story that illustrates the heart of God and how Jesus was an example of that love on earth.

And early in the morning he came again into the temple, and all the people came unto him; and he sat down, and taught them. And the scribes and Pharisees brought unto him a woman taken in adultery; and when they had set her in the midst, They say unto him, Master, this woman was taken in adultery, in the very act. Now Moses in the law commanded us, that such should be stoned: but what sayest thou? This they said, tempting him, that they might have to accuse him. But Jesus stooped down, and with his finger wrote on the ground, as though he heard them not. So when they continued asking him, he lifted up himself, and said unto them, He that is without sin among you, let him first cast a stone at her. And again he stooped down, and wrote on the ground. And they which heard it, being convicted by their own conscience, went out one by one, beginning at the eldest, even unto the last: and Jesus was left alone, and the woman standing in the midst.

124

When Jesus had lifted up himself, and saw none but the woman, he said unto her, Woman, where are those thine accusers? hath no man condemned thee? She said, No man, Lord. And Jesus said unto her, Neither do I condemn thee: go, and sin no more. KJV

The religious leaders brought a woman to Jesus whom they said had been caught "in the very act of adultery". They were going to test Jesus to see what He would do. (I wonder how they found this woman "in the very act"? Perhaps they had set a trap or were peeping toms). Whatever the situation, they brought this woman (probably wrapped in sheet) and asked Jesus what He would do, stating that according to the law (of Moses) she should be stoned to death.

Jesus did not even acknowledge their question but continued writing on the ground. When they persisted He told them that whoever was without sin was to cast the first stone and then continued writing on the ground. The Bible says they were convicted by their own consciences and one by one they all left, from the eldest to the youngest. (I speculate that perhaps the eldest had more sin than the youngest, that's why they left first).

Woman, where are those thine accusers? hath no man condemned thee? (vs 10) When Jesus asked the woman where her accusers were, she answered that they had all left. Notice that Jesus did not call her a prostitute or sinner or degrade her in any way. He called her "woman", giving her back her dignity. And then He declared that he did not accuse her either and she should go and sin no more. *And Jesus said unto her, Neither do I condemn thee: go, and sin no more.* (vs 11)

That is the language of love. It will always restore your self-worth and will always tell you what Jesus has done for you so that you can overcome your sin or moral failure. That is the power of the language of love. It **ENABLES** you to overcome and sin no more.

John 16:12-15 *I have yet many things to say unto you, but ye cannot bear them now. Howbeit when he, the Spirit of truth, is come, he will guide you into all truth: for he shall not speak of himself; but whatsoever he shall hear, that shall he speak: and he will shew you things to come. He shall glorify me: for he shall receive of mine, and shall shew it unto you. All things that the Father hath are mine: therefore said I, that he shall take of mine, and shall shew it unto you.*

The Holy Spirit desires to speak to you and give you direction for your life and to bring you into the fullness intended for you. He will always convince you of your righteousness. Unfortunately like the disciples many of us are not hearing the language of love but are focused on the language of law. The language that God speaks (the language of love) will never point out your mistakes. It will only point out what Jesus has done FOR you and who you are as a result. Even though you have made a horrible mistake, God will not even mention your mistake. He will just remind you that what you are lacking has already been given to you by Jesus.

Jesus came that we might HAVE life. He did not come to LOAN us life. In the scripture He says, "I AM YOUR LIFE, I AM YOUR DELIVERANCE. You see, we are always looking for that "next" experience. But Jesus says, "No, I AM". You don't need another experience. You see the language of love will only tell you who Jesus is for you. He is your righteousness. He is your ability. He is your sanctification. He is everything you need for life. The language of love will ALWAYS tell you who God has made you to be.

Mostly What God Does Is Love You

Now you may be wondering how on earth you are going to overcome all these inabilities in your life. The only way is to become immersed in the fact that God speaks a language of love. So many people think that this message is a license to sin and do just what they please as if there is no control. Well, firstly people have never needed a license to sin and do what they want and secondly they just go about doing whatever they want anyway.

We would never counsel a married couple with difficulties not to love each other too much as it could lead to worse problems. That's like saying, "Don't love your wife too much. She might run away." How stupid! NO! Obviously love will not encourage them to hurt one another. Love will only lead them to appreciate each other more.

How on earth can telling people that God loves them so passionately lead them to more sin? That's ludicrous. You can never tell someone that God loves too much or go "overboard" telling about the love of God. When you find out God loves you so much, you fall in love with him even more and start doing things that you never did before and stop doing some of the things that you did do before. You see you fall in love with Him more and more when you find out that he loves you!

Ephesians 5:1-2 (Message Bible) *"Watch what God does, and then you do it, like children who learn proper behavior from their parents. Mostly what God does is love you. Keep company with him and learn a life of love. Observe how Christ loved us. His love was not cautious but extravagant. He didn't love in order to get something from us but to give everything of himself to us."*

This scripture in the book of Ephesians tell us God's love was not cautious but extravagant. He didn't love us in order to get something FROM us, but to give everything of Himself TO us. The word extravagant means "exceeding the limits of reason or necessity ... lacking in moderation, balance and restraint, extremely or excessively elaborate". What an awesome view of the love God has for us, and why He went to the extreme of the cross to adopt us into His family. The love of God goes beyond whatever your mind can reason or even think of. His love reaches beyond our excuses and failures and draws us into the reality of the life we have been given.

When I fell in love with my wife it changed my life forever. I felt as if my knees had a life of their very own. They wouldn't work right. I started sending her flowers and gifts. I had never done this to any other woman before in my life. And I stopped doing things that I had been doing like having girlfriends in every corner of town or staying out with the boys every night. But none of this was because my wife made a list of 10 things I should and shouldn't do. No it was because I fell IN LOVE with her and she responded to that love.

God's love is so much more than the natural love between a man and a woman. When we find out just how much we are loved by God, it is a natural reaction to respond to that love.

Long before he laid down earth's foundations, he (God) had us in mind, had settled on us as *the focus of his love, to be made whole and holy by his love. Long, long ago he decided to adopt us into his family through Jesus Christ. (**What pleasure he took in planning this!**) He wanted us to enter into the celebration of his lavish gift-giving by the hand of his beloved Son.* Ephesians 1:4 (MSG)

This was the plan from the foundation of the world. Its not a repair job because someone messed up. God the Father, the Son and the Holy Spirit wanted us to share in THEIR life from the very beginning. And it's easy to take hold of and believe that we are part of this wonderful, amazing family. Knowing that we belong, that we "fit", gives us an awesome sense of self-worth and feeling of acceptance.

Take time to learn the language of love because when you do, you will hear God's encouragement every time. It will strengthen and build you up. You will feel good and want to spend time with Him. Your time of fellowship will be wonderful and you will find direction for your life that you have never had before.

Let's take this message of God's unconditional love to everyone. No one has been left out. No one has been excluded. Telling people how bad they are has never helped anyone. Telling someone **good news** makes them feel valuable and wanted and guess what? They become the person they are declared to be! News is something that has already happened ... not something that needs to be done to make it happen! Believing in this good news sets us FREE to feel alive and happy, to enjoy every aspect of life and rest, knowing that we are not under investigation and that God is always part of what we are doing.

For we are God's [own] handiwork (His workmanship), recreated in Christ Jesus, [born anew] that we may do those good works which God predestined (planned beforehand) for us [taking paths which He prepared ahead of time], that we should walk in them [living the good life which He prearranged and made ready for us to live]. Ephesians 2:10 (AMP)

Let the great AWAKENING to His love start with YOU. Right where you are. Your world, your everyday situations need this awakening to the love and life of God the Father, the Son and the Holy Spirit.

My prayer is that this book will start you on the incredible journey to DISCOVER TRUE LOVE and find rest and peace for your soul.